I haven't found myself...
but I'm still looking

Order this book online at www.trafford.com/08-0868
or email orders@trafford.com

Most Trafford titles are also available at major online book retailers.

© Copyright 2008 FESAM.

All rights reserved. No part of this publication may be reproduced, stored in a retrieval system, or transmitted, in any form or by any means, electronic, mechanical, photocopying, recording, or otherwise, without the written prior permission of the author.

Note for Librarians: A cataloguing record for this book is available from Library and Archives Canada at www.collectionscanada.ca/amicus/index-e.html

Printed in Victoria, BC, Canada.

ISBN: 978-1-4251-7765-2

www.trafford.com

North America & international
toll-free: 1 888 232 4444 (USA & Canada)
phone: 250 383 6864 ♦ fax: 250 383 6804
email: info@trafford.com

The United Kingdom & Europe
phone: +44 (0)1865 487 395 ♦ local rate: 0845 230 9601
facsimile: +44 (0)1865 481 507 ♦ email: info.uk@trafford.com

10 9 8 7 6 5 4 3 2

CONTENTS

2...On Autopilot
4...Dealing with Timelines
6...The Purpose of Pain
8...More than Just Words
10...Seasonal Inspiration
12...Energy Conservation
14...Choosing Discomfort
16...Reaching Full Potential
18...The Art of Conversation
20...Mind Over Matter
22...The Real You
24...Action
26...A True Visionary
28...Silence is Golden
30...Natural High
32...Self-Imposed Limitations
34...Green with Envy
36...The Pursuit of Power
38...Just in Time

40...Failure
42...Wasting Time
44...Gratitude
46...Uncertainty
48...Worry Not
50...Mapping It Out
52...Accountability
54...In Good Company
56...Emotional Impact
58...Memories
60...That Little Voice
62...Spiritual Practice
64...Blocked Vessel
66...Body Conscious
68...Passing Judgment
70...Life Is...
72...Moving Up
74...Control Freak
76...The Complete Package
78...The Role of Destiny
80...In the Fog

82...Can You Handle It?
84...Losing It
86...Listen Up
88...Fleeting Desire
90...Inquiring Minds
92...Patient Preparation
94...Authenticity
96...The Beauty of Scars
98...Storybook Endings
100...Buying Time
102...Acceptance
104...Thinking Big
106...Balancing Act
108...Keeping It Real
110...Déjà Vu
112...Tunneling Through
114...Collective Soul
116...Open Spaces
118...Growing Pains
120...Illogical Conclusions
122...Hidden Beliefs

124...Waiting to Bloom
126...Journeys
128...Stuck
130...Insincerity
132...Human Relations
134...Inner Light
136...Doing the Work
138...The Importance of Doubt
140...Glory Days
142...Windswept
144...Fine Dining
146...Nature's Lessons
148...Mixed Signals

Feel free to read the reflections as you wish. Whether randomly or in order, trust that whatever you choose is what your spirit needs at that particular time.

*For my most loyal supporter,
my mother, Agnes*

On Autopilot

We live much of our lives on automatic pilot, and then often ask ourselves, "Why doesn't anything ever change?"

We time ourselves by the daily, weekly, and yearly routines we follow: get children ready for school, catch the bus at 8:15 am, start work at 9:00am, eat lunch at 12:00 p.m., shop for groceries on Saturday, watch sports on Sunday, pay taxes in April...

Whatever the routine, most of us operate our physical bodies based on the workings of our minds. Unfortunately our minds function primarily as scheduling centers. With the busy lives that we lead, it doesn't leave much time or energy for independent thought. So we need to really ask ourselves one thing.

Do we really want something new in life, or do we want the security that routine provides more than we want change?

Once the honest answer is given, then a conscious choice can be made to either accept the immediate circumstances, or to alter some behaviors that can initiate the change sought.

Taking the time to listen to your soul can shed light on where changes can be made if so desired.

When you truly want to make a change, you will do so.

Know that that the Universe will support you in just the way that you need when you are truly ready.

"Life begins at the end of your comfort zone."

- Neale Donald Walsch

Dealing with Timelines

Many of us live our lives with the notion that we must reach certain goals by definitive times. There are several problems with this line of thinking.

First, most timelines we live by have not been self-determined. Society at large dictates when we need to accomplish specific goals. Whether it comes from our families, strangers, or the media, the idea of conformity is consistently reinforced. There's nothing intrinsically wrong - even with society's proposed timeline. The only error is in thinking everyone must adhere to it.

In addition, we often judge ourselves as failures when things don't happen according to plan. While it's important to have a vision of who we want to be and what we want to do, we all can not plot our life happenings down to the second.

If a desire is within your spirit, there must be a way for you to achieve it. Perhaps a slight change in perspective will open up possibilities not yet considered.

Believe that the Universe would not torment you with an aspiration that It had no intention of delivering to you.

There really is a proper time for every thing to happen. Living consciously and listening to that inner voice will open your eyes to what is appropriate and when the time is suitable for you.

"A delay is not a denial."

- Rev. James Cleveland

The Purpose of Pain

Life offers endless opportunities for us to experience the full spectrum of emotion. From the occurrence of a new life or perhaps a spectacular sunset, we feel anything from happiness, to wonder, to a sense of peace and fulfillment.

Unfortunately, from time to time, we also feel the hold of pain and disappointment. At times, the intensity of it can be debilitating.

It is said that time heals all wounds but that is not always the case. Time may allow the initial pain to dissipate, but the effects of it may not completely disappear. It is not uncommon for our difficult experiences to color our perception of how our lives really are. Many of us carry our pain like a cloak and allow it to become an integral part of our characters.

One can claim to be a victim of adversity and operate from that perspective. On the other hand, one can choose to extract something of value from the difficulty.

There's always a lesson to be learned with every experience, good or bad. Keep in mind that the lesson may not provide a reason for the misfortune. The lesson may be something like incidentally discovering an attribute you never knew you possessed such as strength, or tenacity, or integrity.

When you seek the lesson, the pain is lessened.

Time is a passive solution. Reaching for understanding is an active one. How would you rather live? It really is what you make it.

"We must embrace pain and burn it as fuel for our journey."
- Kenji Miyazawa

More than Just Words

Words are powerful.

They not only carry meaning, but they carry much energy. A word is not just a thing. It is an action. It can wound just as easily as it can heal.

It is said that truth hurts, but it is really the manner with which the truth is told. We often refrain from saying things we believe will hurt other people. We know it is socially appropriate to use tact with sensitive matters, and at other times we choose to say nothing at all.

Why is it that the majority of us are more concerned with sparing the feelings of others, but we neglect to afford ourselves the same courtesy? What about the words we use to blame and admonish ourselves? Are they not just as destructive, if not more so, than harsh words uttered to another?

We need to be more conscious of the things we say to ourselves and of ourselves. Seemingly innocuous statements made time and time again wear against our spirits. It is no different than how flowing water over time can etch away rock. Small acts can result in much larger implications for our well-being.

Be mindful of what you are saying to your self. Every word is an action you take upon your soul.

"Words are, of course, the most powerful drug used by mankind."
- Rudyard Kipling

Seasonal Inspiration

With the change of seasons, we are reminded of the cyclical and ephemeral nature of life. Something is present, then it ceases to exist, and another thing comes about.

From a macro perspective, this may be representative of a whole lifetime. A newborn being in the "spring" of her life, an elder being in the "winter" of his. But, on a much smaller scale, seasonal changes can be likened to various periods in our lives. Within a lifetime, each of us will experience countless springs, numerous summers, many autumns, and several winters.

We freely accept the necessity of transition in nature, but we are resistant to apply the same principle to our own lives. Many of us tend to hold steadily onto the past, neglecting the possibility that something better might be up ahead.

A tree can not hold onto its flowers and leaves for fear of losing its treasure. It simply lets go of them knowing that its full beauty will be restored. The same blossoms will not return, but ones that are just as, if not more beautiful than the originals.

Everything comes full circle.

Keeping this principle in mind should allow us to accept change more readily.

Embrace it, for change is equivalent to real living. Anything less is merely existing. There is a vast difference between the two.

Welcome the seasons as they come.

"The known is a prison of past conditioning."

- Deepak Chopra

Energy Conservation

Everything is energy…our thoughts, our words, our actions.

Understanding this principle is essential to overall well-being. Critically thinking about the activities we engage in is crucial. How many times have you left an activity feeling energized? How many times have you left a situation or person feeling completely drained?

The interactions we allow ourselves to become a part of can either enhance or deplete our energy levels. It is mandatory that we learn to protect ourselves in this regard. No one else can or should have to do this for you. Only you are responsible for your energy reserves.

Continually engaging in unfulfilling behaviors is self-defeating. Habitual actions require no thought. Thoughtless actions never strengthen spiritual pursuits.

So why continue to do something if it does not serve your highest self?

One must learn to protect his energy and not allow it to unknowingly dissipate.

Guard your reserves as you would any other valued possession. It is the basis for all that you will be able to do for yourself as well as others.

Living a more conscious life, by making more mindful decisions, will enable you to keep your energy reserves full. And when you are fully energized, the sky's the limit for what you can accomplish.

"Give from your overflow, not from your cup."

- Iyanla Vanzant

Choosing Discomfort

Generally speaking, human beings are creatures of comfort.

Most of us feel some degree of anxiety when there are deviations to our well rehearsed routines. Although the sense of "something is wrong here" serves us well in dangerous situations, it is also the response we have when we willingly depart from what is familiar to us.

At times, our spirits will call for us to do things that are unfamiliar. Challenges put forth in our lives require us to re-examine what we are truly capable of achieving. It is important to recognize that a feeling of uneasiness does not always signal that something is amiss. It may just be the appropriate time to advance in our personal evolution.

Whenever we endeavor to try something new, there is often an element of discomfort. We have to determine whether this feeling is precautionary or if it is just the sensation of adventure beckoning us to step into a new phase of our reality.

Remember that courage is not shown by those who are fearless. Courage is exhibited by those who venture forth despite their fears. Sometimes fear is well-founded, but quite often the fear in our minds far outweighs the reality of the situation.

Facing what is uncomfortable may result in a lasting peace just waiting to be known.

"Comfort is the enemy of achievement."

- Farrah Gray

Reaching Full Potential

How often have you heard or stated the words, "If I could be Oprah for one day…" or "I wish I had one-tenth of Bill Gates' fortune…"

We often look to other people for inspiration. Knowing that someone else has obtained immeasurable success despite overwhelming odds, gives us a sense of optimism.

There's nothing wrong with this practice as long as we use it for motivation, and not for comparison.

It's important to recognize that we are all here to have different experiences. How we approach these individual experiences determines what we make of ourselves in the long run. Each decision made, builds upon the last. At any time, we can make a different decision possibly redirecting the course of our lives.

We tend to unfairly compare ourselves against these icons. We judge ourselves against their most visible triumph, wealth, while disregarding less visible triumphs achieved along our own paths.

We're too busy coveting what we don't have instead of acknowledging what we do have.

Keep in mind that when you strive to achieve someone else's accomplishments, you just might be limiting yourself.

Wouldn't you rather reach 100% of your highest potential instead of a fraction of someone else's?

"Joy comes from using your potential."

- Will Schultz

The Art of Conversation

When was the last time you had an intimate conversation? The type of conversation that speaks of your well-being, your spirit, and the things that really matter? The kind of conversation that speaks to who you really are.

The importance of conversation appears to be disappearing as time moves on. Many blame this phenomenon on the widely accepted use of internet communications. However, this is not truly the root of the problem. In days past, letter writing was widely accepted as a form of genuine communication. The sincerity of an exchange does not depend on the medium, but rather the content.

These days, our conversations are dominated by increasingly mindless material. The details of the latest celebrity divorce is upon the lips of many people, but ask the same people of what feeds their spirits, and no answer is readily available.

People will pay far more attention to the misadventures of famous athletes, than they will to their own personal evolvement. We talk of the latest material trend as if it has a life of its own.

The majority of us are far more intrigued by the stories of other people and things than we are with our own stories. Perhaps it is a way of avoiding our discontent with our own lives.

The usual focal points of your conversations say a lot about what you deem important in your life. Make it a point to include more dialogue about personal growth and matters of the heart. It gets easier to do so once you wholeheartedly believe in your own significance.

"Conversation is an exercise of the mind; gossip is merely an exercise of the tongue."

-unknown

Mind Over Matter

Growing up you may have heard the phrase "Mind your manners." At other times, you were probably told to "Mind your business." But how many times have you heard the phrase "Mind your mind"? And yet this is probably the key to navigating life successfully.

Each day, a human being reportedly has over 50,000 thoughts. A few of these thoughts are probably task oriented such as "I need to make an important phone call…I have to buy groceries." Others are purely observational such as "The traffic light is red." These musings help give order to the day. The overwhelming majority of thoughts, however, are *useless*.

The question becomes, how many thoughts do you have in a day that are negative in nature and directed towards yourself? "I'll never be _____." or "This always happens to me. " These are the thoughts of a victim. They are declarations of the insignificant role you think you play in your own life.

It is said that your thoughts create your reality. So in holding negative beliefs about yourself, you unconsciously reinforce their existence.

The mind does run freely and it may be initially difficult to stop negativity. However, it is important to at least *interrupt* negative thought patterns with more constructive beliefs. Does negativity run rampant through your mind? Only when that fact is acknowledged can it be corrected. Consequently, reality can then be influenced.

Remember, every aspect of your life starts with your thoughts.

Be *mind*-ful.

"Thought is the sculptor who can create the person you want to be."
- Henry David Thoreau

The Real You

Who are you?

We often hear or use the phrase, "I don't know who I am anymore." This is an indication that we feel out of touch with our spirits. The interesting thing is when asked the question, many of us answer based upon characteristics that don't necessarily have any bearing upon who we truly are.

We define ourselves by age, professions, possessions, and relations to other people. For example, "I am a 42 year old father. I live in such and such neighborhood and have practiced medicine for the past ten years." Assumptions may be made about this individual's character, but the truth of the matter is, these are simply roles that have been taken on. Any of these conditions could change without warning.

Too many of us are working on keeping up the façade and allowing it to define who we are to the outside world. Over time, we feel burdened to live by the façade we initially created.

In doing so, we continue to work on the outside, neglecting the inside that so desperately needs attention.

When you ask yourself the question of who you truly are, answers should be based upon inner attributes. Are you loving, compassionate, inquisitive, creative, passionate, tranquil etc...

These are the qualities that reside in your heart, your true essence. These are the things that can never be taken away from you.

So, who are you?

"We define only out of despair; we must have a formula...to give a facade to the void."

— Emile M. Cioran

Action

Generally speaking, we spend much of our time responding to situations that occur. Instead of being proactive and taking an action that may result in a more favorable circumstance, we opt to mindlessly conduct ourselves in a less than pleasant fashion. Living life on the defensive expends much energy and is undoubtedly self-defeating.

Our reaction to unfolding events is not simply a reflex. Often times, it is a literal *re-*action...an action that has been taken many times before. For example, imagine an annoying co-worker or relative. Each time this individual says or does the wrong thing, you may be overcome with anger and retaliate in an inappropriate manner. Such a response is not conducive to the well-being of either party. Your action has served no purpose.

To be living a fully conscious life, you must make an effort to make the best choice in every moment. Consequently, you become the principal character in your own life, actively directing the overall course.

One can not become more attuned with greater possibilities that exist while operating in a habitual manner. Attaining a more spiritual existence requires conscious decision making. How many other areas in your life are you not thinking about your actions?

Choose to **act**, not to re-act.

"Insanity: doing the same thing over and over again and expecting different results."

- Albert Einstein

A True Visionary

Ask most successful individuals how they once envisioned themselves and chances are they believed they were capable of anything and everything. Though their surroundings may have dictated otherwise, they chose to believe only in themselves. They had a vision.

Many of us wish to ascend to the next level whether it is in careers, relationships, or abundance. However, most of us have vague aspirations with no real direction. Because you have a desire, does not mean you have vision. Vision is what provides clarity for your intended destination.

Along with authentic vision must come determination. All too often, we tend to look outside of ourselves for reinforcement. If positive feedback is not readily available, one can easily succumb to the urge to simply give up. With real vision, the only barometer for success comes from within. There is an internal reference point called spirit.

You have to remember that the way you look at the world is specific to you - physically and mentally.

Imagine you and a friend are looking at an object in the distance. The two of you are separated by fifty feet. Though you are looking at the same thing, you each see differently because your physical perspective is unique.

The same rule applies to what your mind envisions. The next person can not "see" the identical images you hold because his viewpoint/mentality is his alone.

Vision is *personal*. What do you "see" for yourself?

"A man's dreams are an index to his greatness."

- Zadok Rabinowitz

Silence is Golden

The importance of silence is being overshadowed by the ways of daily existence. Television, cellular phones, games, internet surfing…there are endless methods of distraction suited to a variety of personalities.

Then there are those of us who prefer to read a book or listen to music. These activities can also be considered distractions in that we are still involved with something outside of ourselves. Granted, many of these activities can aid spiritual growth, but none should preclude silence itself.

For many individuals this is an uncomfortable practice equated with experiencing boredom or "wasting valuable time". But that is only because they do not see what is to be gained.

Many times we turn to distractions rather than address current difficulties or stresses. In silence, we can become more attuned to spirit and can pinpoint our real needs.

It is also in these periods we are able to access our intuition most easily. Sometimes the answers we so desperately seek are completely within.

We're so busy looking outwards for the next thing to do, we forget to use the inherent wisdom we each possess.

Incorporating a period of silence into your daily routine can cultivate a more conscious way of living. It helps to center thoughts and foster clarity of purpose.

When was the last time you made a deliberate effort to just be still and listen?

"Talking comes by nature, silence by wisdom."

- unknown

Natural High

We all experience moments when we feel particularly vibrant or what some may describe as a "natural high". It is crucial to our well-being to feel full of life. However, what brings about an energetic temperament is something that should be closely examined.

Many of us engage in neutral activities that provide immediate but brief pleasure. The acquisition of material items provides such an example. Many of us do not treat ourselves because we deem ourselves worthy, but rather we believe that having a particular item gives us our value. The "high" that is obtained is tainted with false belief.

Others of us feel most alive when engaged in destructive activities. These are the individuals who derive satisfaction from belittling others. Whether it's "road rage" or a tyrannical boss, the same objective is met...to wage war and subsequently win the battle.

Note that the flame of a lit candle when used to light another candle does not cease to exist. And so it should be when two individuals have an exchange. One never has to gain power at the expense of another.

Authentic highs result when you are engaged in something that resonates with your spirit. There is no aspect of ego involved. Helping a person in need, creating a work of art, appreciating beauty, etc…are all examples of this. Fulfillment is derived from the purity of the activity.

What makes you feel full of life? Are you feeding your spirit or are you feeding something else?

"Spirit is fueled by acts of substance."

- unknown

Self-Imposed Limitations

How many times does the phrase "I can't" enter your thoughts or your conversations? Two little words which hold a tremendous amount of power.

When you tell yourself that you don't have the ability to achieve a goal, you shortchange yourself. What separates you from the person on the next level who has achieved that goal? Is that person more dedicated, more intelligent, or more appealing than you perceive yourself to be?

We all have inherent strengths and other attributes that just need to be strengthened. A weakness remains just that only if it is not worked upon.

Perhaps sitting back and declaring those limitations provides an excuse for not bothering to try. Is it possible you tell yourself you can't just so you don't have to expend the energy? For others, it may be easier to negate your ability rather than admit your fear of possible failure.

Whether inaction is due to laziness or apprehension makes no real difference. The end result is the same. There is no progress.

Until you work up to the next level, you have no idea of your true capabilities. The quest to find out should be unending. When you are in touch with spirit, your potential is infinite. Every time you utter the words "I can't", you miss an opportunity for greater growth.

What self-imposed limitations do you hold?

"Why when God's earth is so wide, have you fallen asleep in a prison?"

- Rumi

Green with Envy

The desire to maintain pace with our peers i.e. "keeping up with the Joneses" can be overwhelming. Depending on where an individual resides, one may be bombarded with continual images of outward perfection.

The media tells us that our houses aren't big enough, our clothes aren't fashionable enough, our appearance isn't pleasing enough. Unfortunately, these myths become our truths. Once the "truth" is internalized, we tend to look outward further affirming the belief that we need more.

This is the reason that going within is of crucial importance. When we continually look outside of ourselves for cues as to what we consider "completion", we lose perspective on the things that feed our well-being.

Material things need not be given up, but they should not take precedence over the development of your spirit. Otherwise, you end up with a beautifully decorated empty shell.

As you begin to realize your full value, the desire to "keep up" with others will slowly dissipate. Remember, in any race, looking left and right only slows your pace. Focus straight ahead on your own journey and your progress will be that much swifter.

Life is not a typical race to be run with other competitors. The measure of success is not based on place or time. It is an individual's pursuit of their best self. The pace of evolution is entirely up to you.

"Envy is the art of counting the other fellow's blessings instead of your own."

- Harold Coffin

The Pursuit of Power

When we think of people who are powerful, we often conjure up images of individuals who yield undeniable authority. These are the people who make their presence known, voice their opinions, and get things done.

Powerful people are often larger than life and it is difficult for the "average" person to see his or herself in the same light. Because one may not have this particular type of personality, it is easy to identify with feeling powerless.

But not all of us are meant to exercise power in the same way. We all have it, but we simply express it differently. Those of us who feel incapable can always learn to cultivate it. And those of us who naturally display such dominance, need not do so in all situations.

Exhibiting power does not always call for outward and immediate action. Sometimes, the greatest strength you have is to hold still and go within. There can be infinite power in appropriate restraint.

When you feel powerless, it is because you are in a place of doubt. This only signals that you are not connected with spirit. Find a personal way to reconnect (journal, meditate, pray, exercise, etc...) and your sense of power will return. It is then you decide whether action is necessary or not.

Calling upon your innate power is a conscious choice you make. Once you realize that, you will never truly feel powerless again.

"Our deepest fear is not that we are inadequate. Our deepest fear is that we are powerful beyond measure."

- Marianne Williamson

Just in Time

How often have we breathed a sigh of relief when a precarious situation turned out just fine?

Perhaps the rain started to pour down just as shelter was reached. Or maybe a check came just in time to cover an unexpected expense. Or maybe the perfect individual showed up with the right information or the perfect opportunity.

We tend to forget how many times things have worked out in our favor when we least expected it to do so. We're acutely aware of our disappointment when things don't work out according to our *own* schedules. We tend to feel abandoned. But in reality, we're never truly alone.

The only thing that is within our control is to make the best possible decision at every turn with the guidance of spirit.

To do so, one must act with purpose and not move through the world unconsciously as so many of us do. The rest of the details have to be left up to a greater force.

We have such a limited perspective on what a perfect outcome entails. As one piece in an infinite puzzle, it is impossible for us to know exactly how we are contributing to and being supported by the bigger picture.

Universal timing is impeccable. Trust in its infallibility.

"Time is just God's way of making sure that everything doesn't happen all at once."

— George Carlin

Failure

We've all heard the axiom "If at first you don't succeed, then try, try, again."

It reinforces the idea that failing will often precede success.

Instead of taking this to heart, many of us associate failure with several negative connotations. We believe that it somehow defines us and speaks to the impossibility of altering our futures. As a result, we either lower our standards ensuring a "success" of sorts, or we refuse to try at all thereby avoiding the chance of failure.

We need to revise our perspectives on what failing actually is. Perhaps we should think of it as a temporary state in which to re-assess and fine tune our strategies to achieve.

As many accomplished individuals will reveal, they, too, have experienced falling short of their proposed ideals somewhere along the line.

The difference with them is that they refused to internalize it. Why? Because surrendering to defeat is inconsistent with the nature of spirit.

A fear of failure is a covert declaration of incompetence. Being in touch with your spirit erases the concept of limitations. Failing is merely an opportunity for something greater. Accept the challenge to rise.

"There is no failure except in no longer trying."

- Elbert Hubbard

Wasting Time

"I'll just wait until…"

How often do we delay an experience or some course of action because we assume we'll get to it later? In the meantime, we engage in fruitless activities that fail to yield any benefits.

We say we'll begin a healthier lifestyle *next* week, but continue to neglect our physical and mental condition *now*. We promise to indulge ourselves *after* retirement, but work at a detrimental pace in the interim. We talk of pursuing our passions *some day*, but continually suppress the present desire. In each instance, there is little regard for spirit.

The comfort of familiarity is powerful. All too often, we are lulled into complacency with the moment. Before we know it, so much time has passed that the opportunity we put on hold has passed us by.

Think of each second as a seed of potential. Indefinitely postponing proposed goals allows these seeds to slip through our hands. It amounts to discarding pieces of the soul while hoping for some sense of gratification in the future.

We can not suspend time. Why keep suspending fulfillment?

Now is the only thing that is real. Give yourself permission to enjoy this moment.

"If we are to better the future, we must disturb the present."
- Catherine Booth

Gratitude

It is often stressed that having an attitude of gratitude is essential to allow further blessings into one's life.

It's easy to be grateful for the good in our lives when things are going well. For most of us, however, it's difficult to do so in times of trouble. Sorrow obscures our clarity of vision. It often detaches us from our source of strength which is spirit.

It is during hardship when we truly find out how connected we are to our cores. People often speak of their faith (religious or otherwise) but it is during these times when it has to be demonstrated.

Perhaps, changing the perspective from which we view our tribulations can help alleviate the angst. It's natural to experience doubt and worry initially, but if we can catch ourselves in the process, we can modify the direction in which we are headed.

Instead of fully succumbing to the grief, it is possible to see the situation as an opportunity for renewal of faith.

If we can recollect all the wonders that have previously turned up, not only do we maintain an attitude of gratitude, but we also reassure ourselves of the possibility of miracles.

Gratitude not only leads to other blessings, but in helping us to heal is a blessing in itself.

"The hardest arithmetic to master is that which enables us to count our blessings."

- Eric Hoffer

Uncertainty

Delving into uncertainty is challenging for the majority of us. We like to know what's ahead of us, if possible.

When we come to significant crossroads in life, we have a tendency to choose the familiar. But even with the most trivial of decisions, we tend to stick with the same choices. Often times, we call them preferences, but the truth is we rarely try alternatives to know what we truly *prefer*.

There's nothing inherently wrong with always doing the same thing…if it works for you. However, many of us continue to make the same choices despite the discontent that may accompany them.

Start making minor decisions that may feel a little uncomfortable. For example, wear a different color than usual, or choose a new brand of cereal. Consciously exploring inconsequential alternatives may serve as practice for facing larger turning points in life.

Should the proverbial fork in the road occur, making the uncomfortable choice may not feel as foreign.

Life is too short to have the same experience over and over again. Life may be too long to have the same experience over and over again.

What's the point of all your tomorrows being just like yesterday?

"Man cannot discover new oceans unless he has the courage to lose sight of the shore."

- Andre Gide

Worry Not

The world is a vast place with an infinite number of challenges. In our immediate environment, not only are there various personal issues to be dealt with, but there are the issues of those that are close to us. Beyond our concerns, lie those of billions of others.

In this sea of complexity, our own worries may appear insignificant. Resolutions may not be forthcoming and doubt can settle in. It's easy to feel forgotten and abandoned.

It is often said that everything happens for a reason. When there isn't an apparent reason, we begin to wonder if this is so. Operating apart from spirit leaves us feeling like our trials are random in nature.

If we take the time to think of the happenings around us, we would realize that much of the world works in a very orderly manner. Even something as tiny as a snowflake has a precise structure. The ice crystals come together to create incredibly beautiful arrangements. Why create such intricate splendor on only a small level?

The next time the odds seem stacked against you, remember that if the minutest details are taken care of, the same principle probably applies to your own life.

Do everything to the best of your ability and trust in the order and the reasoning of the Universe to take care of the rest.

"Worry gives a small thing a big shadow."

- Swedish proverb

Mapping It Out

No matter at which level we find ourselves in our personal development, there is always room for improvement.

Just as we refer to a map when we're moving into foreign territory, we must apply the same principle to our spiritual journeys. In order to get to your intended destination, you have to first accurately determine where you are. Only then can you determine how far you have to go. Unfortunately, this is a step that so many of us fail to do.

Evaluating one's current position can be an uncomfortable experience. We don't like to willingly reveal our flaws and face them head on. On a day to day basis, we hide our shortcomings from the people around us. But far more detrimental is the way we do the same thing to ourselves.

We pretend we're being carefree when the truth is we're acting irresponsibly. We place blame on external forces for situations we know we brought on ourselves.

We convince ourselves we're content rather than admitting things should be better than they are.

Self-deceit is incompatible with personal growth. We must acknowledge our innermost challenges before we are able to overcome them.

As long as we hide from the truth, our progress will remain limited. When charting your spiritual course, remember that a map is a useless tool if the starting point is unclear.

"You never find yourself until you face the truth."

- Pearl Bailey

Accountability

In today's society, the "blame game" has become more than commonplace. Parents are blamed for our adult neuroses. Television is blamed for our declining physical inactivity. Lawsuits for trivial matters are exponentially growing in number.

It appears that we have traded in accountability for the convenient role of victimization. The majority of us are especially reluctant to implicate ourselves in our own adversities.

Like any activity that is worthwhile, introspection requires work. There is no involved effort when we hold forces outside of ourselves responsible for our situations. The unwillingness to look within is a display of unconscious behavior.

Individuals who are serious about their spiritual progress will always look to themselves first to see what part they have played in every situation. They do not seek credit nor do they relentlessly blame themselves.

The only objective is to consciously evaluate their motives for engaging or not engaging in some action. That revelation will then serve as a reference for the next similar experience.

By holding yourself accountable for the consequences of your decisions, you gain control of your situation. Accountability is an essential part of growth. Looking outside renders you powerless.

Look inside and reclaim your power.

"Accountability breeds response-ability."

- Stephen R. Covey

In Good Company

Humans can not thrive in isolation. Our well-being depends on our healthy interactions with others. The existence of "feral children" and the detrimental effects of adult solitary confinement confirm this. We need human contact.

For many of us, our families and friends provide this. Our physical and mental needs are met by these interactions, but this is not always enough. It is imperative to take note of our spiritual well-being.

Staying focused on the things that matter can sometimes be challenging. This is even more difficult when trying to do so alone. The voices of ego and society are often louder than our own.

Keeping trusted people around you is vital. Their influences can not help but color your outlook on life and your approach to living. These are the people who encourage the best from you, but do not judge you for falling short.

Not everyone who is in your life can contribute to the highest interests of your soul. Make sure that your inner circle is comprised of individuals who have the ability to support your spiritual interests, and for whom you can do the same.

Remember that the state of your spirit is often mirrored back to you by the people who surround you.

"Tell me what company you keep and I'll tell you what you are."
- Miguel de Cervantes

Emotional Impact

Imagine a stranger's reaction should you choose to answer the question "How are you?" with an honest answer on a bad day. Most of us have learned to present a neutral or happy disposition when interacting with others. Given society's rules of etiquette, it's no surprise that many of us tend to repress our emotions…even to ourselves.

On the other hand, there are those of us who ride the ups and downs and everyone around us knows it. One moment, all is well then in the blink of an eye, anger can overtake a situation. Some of us allow emotions to overwhelm us.

Whether it is repression or unbridled expression that takes place, neither approach is truly beneficial. However, it is important to always acknowledge what is felt. Emotions are accurate measures of one's overall well-being.

Being overly sensitive or decidedly detached indicates a need for further self-exploration. Operating from a spiritual perspective requires the ability to separate from the pull of human tendencies.

To be fully conscious, one has to observe oneself from a neutral perspective. Stepping out of the moment to assess a situation takes great discipline and much practice.

Whether it's a hint of emotion or a full-blown feeling, be sure to pay attention. Emotion always gives insight to much deeper dynamics. The real reasons we feel the way we do have more to do with what's inside of us than what is outside.

"Let's not forget that the little emotions are the great captains of our lives and we obey them without realizing it."

- Vincent Van Gogh

Memories

Memories can provide a sweet reprieve from mundane or troubled times. But sometimes the appeal of reminiscing gets in the way of constructive action.

Good memories can be like security blankets. They offer immediate comfort but also encourage a sort of dependency. Instead of simply reminding us of the blessings we've had before and are sure to experience again, we often get caught up in wishing for the past. Some of us go as far as to try and re-create it.

No matter how incredible past moments may have been, trying to re-live the same experiences goes against the nature of spirit. Acceptance of change is part of what defines spirit. It is always in search of progress.

Immersing oneself in memories can interfere with that progress. Why? Because this practice can interfere with imagination.

We sometimes settle for the *feel* of a memory, instead of creating a real time experience. While reminiscing, we neglect the possibilities of the present moment.

How much of you is living for now and how much of you is submerged in the past? Remember that you can only explore the possibilities when you first imagine what they are.

You can not open yourself to receive when your hands and heart are full with things of the past.

"Imagination is everything. It is the preview of life's coming attractions."
- Albert Einstein

That Little Voice

We've all heard that little voice in the back of our heads. It's our built-in navigation system that lets us know when we're heading off-track. Unfortunately, we don't always listen.

How many times has an opportunity been missed or an unfavorable event taken place and we immediately think, "Something told me I should have…" Having had that experience more than once, why is it that we don't automatically heed our intuition?

Sometimes doing what our spirit requires of us takes work. It can call us to do what seems impossible and feels uncomfortable. Sometimes it goes against everything else that the outside world is saying. In short, listening to and following that voice is not always easy.

A less demanding response is to ignore the voice and take what appears to be an easier way out. We create a less than ideal situation despite our best instincts and call it a sacrifice.

Granted at times, sacrifices do have to be made. But in cases like these, the "sacrifice" is born out of fear or avoidance, and not out of necessity. Consequently, the little voice gets louder.

Take some time to listen to your true voice. It not only reflects your conscience but is also your gauge of authenticity. Is your manner of living consistent with who you are at your core?

"Intuition is a spiritual faculty and does not explain, but simply points the way."

- Florence Scovel Shinn

Spiritual Practice

It is commonly said that we are spiritual beings having a human experience. Unfortunately, the majority of us get caught up living in the opposite manner.

The demands of mere survival heavily dictate our moment to moment interactions. With all the pressures of daily existence in a modern world, it's challenging to live in constant awareness of one's spirit. Those of us living in urban areas are that much further removed from reminders of the "important things." So how is it possible to make an earnest attempt at soulful living?

For all activities considered worthwhile, conscious effort is required. Spirituality is no different. For example, an athlete makes a choice each day to practice his or her sport. The resultant benefits become apparent over time. The practice becomes easier and competence increases.

This same approach should be taken into consideration when developing one's spiritual practice. Many of us try activities such as meditation, yoga, or journaling.

Far too often, we become discouraged by not seeing the immediate results of well-being. Consequently we discontinue the practice long before any improvements have had a chance to manifest.

Remember that each day you make a choice to acknowledge your spirit. Its development is completely within your control. Your "human-ness" should not eclipse your true self.

"We are not human beings on a spiritual journey. We are spiritual beings on a human journey."

- Stephen R. Covey

Blocked Vessel

Life is full of ups and downs. Much of how we experience these cycles has to do with which part of us is engaged in the process. In other words, through whose eyes are we witnessing the situation – ego or spirit? Difficult times tend to reveal which part of us is stronger.

When we hit times of crisis, the grip of panic often takes hold. We see nothing other than the "horrible ordeal" that is happening *to* us. When we're under its influence, we are unable to envision a way out and some of us resign ourselves to the worst possible outcome. It is apparent that in these instances we are operating from the perspective of ego.

Conversely, spirit always maintains the highest hopes but understands that whatever the outcome, it can be dealt with. A person who thinks consciously is always aware of this fact. They are able to recognize that panic obscures their clarity.

Think of yourself as a vessel receiving input from the Universe. When panic takes over, your interior is quickly filled with fear and doubt. There is no room for a solution. Spirit is clear of these burdens. Only an open vessel can accept an alternative outlook.

Recognize the ego's panic for what it truly is…a signal that the spirit needs strengthening.

"You can never solve a problem on the level on which it was created."
- Albert Einstein

Body Conscious

We often look outside of ourselves for signs of a greater force. We take in stars and marvel at their existence. We hear of miracles and it reinforces our belief in something greater.

But the reality is that we habitually ignore the wonder that is with us at all times. We ignore our selves…our physical bodies. It is easy to take for granted the gift that we have been given – especially if it is in working order. It is only when illness or disability comes upon us that we stop and think of our own constitution.

Though it is important to strengthen the spirit, it is also important to acknowledge our physicality. We frequently adorn the outside but we often forget about the inner workings. Being that we are so often focused on that which is outside of us, perhaps the things we see can serve as reminders of the intricacy of our physical nature.
A thing as simple as veins on leaves of a plant can be a reminder of the vessels that run through each of us to nourish our bodies.

That trillions of our cells can be attended to by this complicated network is something to be revered.

The next time you see lightning in the sky, remember that there is actual voltage running through you on a regular basis. It is how your heart functions and how your brain communicates with each part of you. There is figuratively and literally energy running within.

Learn to respect the entity that houses your spirit. Contemplating its complex makeup should be evidence enough that there is something greater at work.

"The body is a sacred garment."

- Martha Graham

Passing Judgment

It is easy to sit back and point out all the "wrongs" that we see. We wonder why others can't be more civil, patient, or rational. It is rare for any of us to fully accept people as they are. Most of us live in a perpetual state of judgment.

It is difficult to avoid being judgmental seeing as how we ourselves are constantly critiqued. We receive grades at school. We are given evaluations at traditional jobs.

Society gives us norms and averages we try to place ourselves within. We strive to be "acceptable". When we witness someone else who is outside of that, we make a mental note. The transient superiority we might feel is illusory. Being judgmental eats away at spiritual reserves.

People who are spiritually evolved are not concerned with assessing others. They understand that everyone is on a different track.

We all have varying experiences and just as many interpretations. It's unfair to judge another by one's own standards.

Spiritual progress is an independent pursuit. People who are truly on a spiritual journey, compare themselves to who they used to be, not to other people. Therefore, judgment becomes an unnecessary activity.

The next time you feel the impulse to judge, remember that it is likely someone else is evaluating you. Quite possibly, you may not agree with their critique. Wouldn't you prefer them to give you the benefit of the doubt? If so, can you not extend that same courtesy to another?

"We can never judge the lives of others, because each person knows only their own pain and renunciation. It's one thing to feel that you are on the right path, but it's another to think that yours is the only path."
- Paulo Coelho

Life is...

When troubling times occur, people will often say, "That's just the way life is." Although there may be some truth in that statement, it is largely inaccurate. It suggests that life is problematic. There is an air of negativity to this point of view.

Will the same person who utters "that's just the way life is" say the same thing during good times? Probably not. The tendency to gravitate towards and dwell on the negative is unfortunately common.

Much of our attitude towards life is largely dictated by our chosen perspective and not necessarily by what takes place. When we continuously grumble that life is just difficult, we are really exhibiting a response of victimization.

It suggests that there is no personal power and one must just withstand the problem at hand. A spiritually aware individual accepts no such limitations. Such a standpoint can not enrich the soul.

Perhaps it is advantageous for us to view life as happening with us rather than to us. Is it possible that we influence our experience of life simply by our outlook on it? This is not to say that all difficulty can be avoided by only thinking positive. It does, however, change our experience of that difficulty.

Life is difficult at times, but for most of us it is also surprising and often cheerful. To ignore the array of life's possibilities is to disrespect its wondrous nature.

Have you examined your dominant opinion of what life entails?

"The soul is dyed the color of your thoughts."

- Herculitus

Moving Up

Spiritual lessons can always be derived from everyday activity. Applying the same principles to mental well-being as is done in the physical world can be greatly rewarding. Such is the act of moving.

Most people dread moving because of the tremendous amount of work involved. There is little difference with moving to a higher level of spirituality. There is no easy path and many choose to remain where they are because it is effortless. Unfortunately, they penalize themselves by missing out on what could have been.

For those that decide a move is imperative, only essential elements should be taken. Figuring out what is necessary and what is not is often unclear. Emotion plays a huge role in being unable to release extraneous baggage.

Travel is faster with a lighter load. Remember that traveling with the same items only allows you to move into the same situation.

What's the point of moving in the same plane of existence… physically or mentally?

Once the initial move is complete, the lightness of the new environment can be overwhelming. There are no comfortable surroundings to encourage a relapse into the previous reality. One is forced to create a new way of operating in this new space. This is no different from entering into a higher mindset. Fresh approaches must be taken on one at a time while furnishing a novel perspective.

There's a big difference between merely moving and moving up. Which way is your spiritual well-being headed?

"I find the great thing in this world is not so much where we stand, as in what direction we are moving."

– Oliver Wendell Holmes

Control Freak

The illusion of control has much influence over many of our actions. We like to think we are in complete charge of our destinies. Granted, our thoughts and desires influence our futures, but it's important to recognize the role that the Universe plays as well.

Chances are that if we were in complete control of our lives, the majority of us would choose to experience the same things. Known outcomes are preferred by most people. We tend not to venture too far outside of our comfort zones.

This is the beauty of the universe. Its unpredictability allows for us to encounter new experiences. It can push us to engage in ways we never imagined. Whether we choose to embrace or repel the unexpected circumstance is entirely up to each of us.

Efforts to control every detail in our lives work against this natural process. Our only responsibility is to do what we can to the best of our abilities and then simply let go.

Keep in mind that the Universe is able to orchestrate events that you can not possibly foresee. In order to allow the Universe to work its wonder, we must permit some room for variation.

We should treat our lives somewhat like we do the weather. We have some idea of what to expect and try to prepare for it. We accept that we can't control it, but we can act accordingly should circumstances change unexpectedly.

The spiritual response is to adapt. The unconscious one is to control.

"Life is what happens when you're busy making other plans."

- John Lennon

The Complete Package

We often tell ourselves that when we obtain that last thing, then we'll be complete. Whether it's a significant other, a child, a home, a job, etc...the lack of some thing is often viewed as a deficiency. Many of us believe we can not go to the next level without the coveted thing.

The problem with this point of view is that completion can never be obtained. There will always be something else to acquire. Perhaps our definition of completion should be revised.

Perhaps completion isn't even a quality we should be pursuing. Maybe betterment or elevation of spirit is a more worthy goal. Trying to obtain completion in the traditional sense will always leave us at the mercy of that which is outside of us.

Completion is something that should be an inner aspiration. Maybe the purpose of our existence is that we only work *towards* that "completion." Any other definition is one that is illusory.

Imagine a car that has no steering wheel. The exterior may be incredibly attractive, but what good is it? It is unable to head in any direction. Its means of navigation is absent. Why should life view you any differently?

When a situation presents itself and you show up devoid of spirit, why should you expect to advance? You have no means of navigating through a new circumstance.

Life requires that your spirit is constantly moving towards wholeness. The only things you have to complete are each of the individual steps on the way up.

"What saves a man is to take a step. Then another step."
- Antoine de Saint-Exupery

The Role of Destiny

People often talk of destiny. She was destined to meet that one person…he was destined to be a CEO, they were destined to be rich, etc…

But in speaking of destiny, some of us will lazily sit back and wait for the world to take care of our problems without any effort on our part. We can make bad decisions or no decisions and assume things will work out as fate would have it.

Others with a more pessimistic view may not even try believing that there is nothing that can be done to avoid an ill fate. Either way, these perspectives disregard the importance of accountability.

Allowing destiny to play a role as opposed to solely depending on it are two very different things. The truth is that no matter what we believe, none of us knows for certain. But why not take a proactive role rather than a passive one?

Maybe our experiences here are supposed to be the interplay of actions based on spirit and options presented by destiny.

What if we viewed life as a perpetual puzzle? As each piece falls into place, imagine that the picture slightly changes. That way, the end result is always flexible.

If we were able to see the finished picture before the puzzle was complete, wouldn't that make life a little dreary?

Perhaps we shouldn't view destiny as so final. Maybe destiny is a collection of possibilities for an individual life. With that outlook, anything is still possible.

"It is in your moments of decision that your destiny is shaped."
- Anthony Robbins

In the Fog

There are times in our lives when we feel we are doing all that we can. We feel in touch with our spirit's desires. Clear intentions have been delineated. Our actions appear to be in line with our highest possible ideals. And yet, something feels amiss.

Ascension to the next level appears to be taking longer than necessary. A fog settles in and we become unsure of which steps to take next. Waiting for the fog to lift requires much patience. There are several reasons that the fog may exist.

Perhaps the development of certain skills or attributes is the reason things are the way they are. Maybe a lesson in patience itself is the purpose. Maybe this temporary state is an exercise in faith and knowing.

A second alternative may be that the extra time provides a period for re-assessment of your current consciousness. What are your motives for your actions? Are they still in line with your best intentions?

A third alternative may have little to do with you. Perhaps the world still needs preparation time for your arrival. Certain conditions may have to be in place before your "time" can occur.

In the meantime we feel at a loss not seeing what's ahead and not understanding what has passed. In a fog there is complete disorientation and all we can do is slowly but steadily move forward.

People with vision know where they want to go but they don't necessarily see exactly how they are going to get there. Keep that in mind and wait with assuredness that all is just as it should be.

Fog always dissipates.

"It is not the clear-sighted who rule the world. Great achievements are accomplished in a blessed, warm fog."

-Joseph Conrad

Can You Handle It?

It is often said that we are only given as much as we can handle. We tend to remember this axiom when we are in times of trouble. It encourages us to push on despite the weakness we may feel.

But how often do we think of this saying in other situations? When we feel stagnancy in our lives, do we stop to consider that perhaps we can not handle anything better?

We assume that should all our wishes come to be, all would be well and we could go on living happily ever after. But what if that coveted job promotion ends up putting a strain on intimate relationships? What if a new love interest is jeopardized because you still have issues with trust?

What if the very thing you want will cause more confusion than you can envision?

Imagine you have a ten year old child in your care. You want to give the child a reasonable allowance. Would it make sense to give this child five thousand dollars on a weekly basis?

In most cases, this would not be deemed appropriate. The child does not possess the maturity or foresight to deal with the amount given. As the child demonstrates responsibility and sound judgment, the allowance can be increased accordingly. Perhaps life is waiting for our growth before increasing our rewards.

Are you truly prepared to receive the things you say you want? If not, why should the universe invest in something that you will undoubtedly squander?

"The human spirit will not invest in mediocrity."

- James Arthur Ray

Losing It

We often think of the word "loss" as being something negative. It suggests a defeat of some sort.

Conversely we associate the word "gain" as being something positive. Generally speaking, the more we are able to acquire the better off we feel we are. But the reality is that loss and gain are really counterparts, not opposites.

When we believe we are losing something we've become comfortable with, the urge to resist is strong. Without truly thinking about what we are doing, many of us fight for things that serve no real purpose.

We fight to preserve non-nurturing relationships. We resist letting go of destructive behaviors and habits. We hold onto distorted beliefs about the way the world operates.

Sometimes losing even the negative aspects of our lives can be distressing.

We become comfortable with the discomfort; hence the struggle to retain that which is actually restricting our maximum potential.

In order for our spirits to grow, we must liberate ourselves from many things. Sometimes, it's freeing our selves from limiting thought patterns. Other times, it may be breaking away from negative influences be it people or situations.

Regardless of our individual paths, we will all leave several things behind along the way. Our job is to accept what falls away with the assurance that we are gaining something much more valuable.

What do you have to lose?

"Loss is nothing else but change, and change is Nature's delight."
- Marcus Aurelius

Listen Up

Sharing our personal truths is not an easy feat. This is especially so when those truths are in conflict with that of another party. Effective communication is an art that the majority of us never truly master. We tend to speak more than we listen and as a result, our intended messages are frequently lost.

Real listening can be made difficult by all the static that surrounds us. We hear the demands of our own egos. We may also be subjected to the wrath of the other person's ego. In addition, we may have to deal with third party opinions and suggestions.

These external and internal influences can color our rationale. Our truths become blurred in the process. As a result, our attempts at communication are flawed. Instead of being consciously chosen, our words emerge from emotion. They no longer have a spiritual basis.

Listening to the other party we are trying to reach is essential, but more importantly, we have to listen to our true selves before we even think to speak.

Before important communications, it is imperative we have a clear understanding of what our intentions are.

When you speak from the spirit, the message is bound to have more clarity. When you speak from any place else, the authenticity of your remarks are lost. More likely than not, your words will not lead to a desirable outcome.

In order to speak your truth, you have to uncover it first.

"Communication is depositing a part of yourself in another person."
- unknown

Fleeting Desire

We've all experienced lightness in our being when we're exposed to something that resonates with us. It's in those moments we experience real joy. All is forgotten except for what is taking place at that instant. We are fully immersed in the "now". But how often do we suppress the opportunity to plunge into that feeling?

We've all felt inklings of desire to engage in some action. But just as soon as such an idea emerges, we dismiss those fleeting thoughts as being silly. We tell ourselves things like "I'm too old", or "What will people think", etc... and talk ourselves out of the idea before it comes to full fruition.

What if those passing moments are life's invitation to experience more of the joy that we seek? Opportunity keeps coming right to our door and we refuse to let it in.

The next time an idea comes to you that feels uplifting for some unknown reason, make sure to follow up on it. Perhaps that exact activity may not be entirely appropriate, but some derivative of it may make more sense for your lifestyle. For example, you may not become a lead ballerina at 65, but you can still take an adult dance class.

It is said in many places that spirit whispers. Its power is likely to show up in a subtle manner. We must pay attention to those subtleties. Following our desires honors our spirits. Note that this does not refer to material desires, but those that help expand the definition of self.

Are you listening to your soul's desires? Are you welcoming joy into your life?

"Desire is God tapping at the door of your mind, trying to give you greater good."

- Catherine Ponder

Inquiring Minds

It is difficult to remember our individuality, when so much of our world insists on sameness. People tend to caution us when we test our boundaries. They say things like, "No one's ever done that before" and "I don't think that's a good idea."

Many a time, these phrases aren't necessarily said out of concern, but out of the other person's own fear. They would never take your intended route because the thought is too overwhelming - for *them*...not you. This is why it's so important to keep conscious of what you are being told and to consistently question the validity of what is said.

A habit of questioning does not have to belligerent or confrontational. It doesn't even have to be said aloud. It can be completely internal so as not to ruffle the feathers of those unable to consider your point of view.

Questioning things is merely a way of gaining insight into who you are and what you really stand for. By doing so, you cultivate an awareness for what truly moves you.

There is no adoption of ideas and attitudes that may be counter to your spirit. Questioning allows you to make the highest decision for your own well being. Consequently, harmonious results usually arise for you and those around you.

Great discoveries and creations are often made by pioneers who dare to step away from the masses. In doing so, the noise of sameness is lessened. They can listen to their own spirits.

Falling unconsciously into line with the masses will only lead to a "soul-less" existence. Are you creating your path, or are you willingly accepting someone else's reality as your own?

"The power to question is the basis of all human progress."
-Indira Gandhi

Patient Preparation

It is said that "good things come to those who wait." Sometimes it feels as if we are endlessly waiting for something to happen. But how often do we use the extra time to our advantage? Do we even think to prepare for the arrival of what we wait for?

We believe that patience is all it takes. But the appearance of something new in our lives usually requires us to be more proactive. Perhaps the interval is solely for that purpose.

Imagine receiving guests into your home. Chances are a thorough cleaning of the space they will occupy will be performed. In addition to clearing space out, we place items we anticipate our guests will need. We do whatever is necessary for them to feel comfortable while they are in our direct care.

Perhaps we need to view our wishes and intentions in the same light. Before they can comfortably fit into our space, we must act accordingly anticipating their arrival.

Mental clutter needs to be addressed. A thorough cleansing of our belief system is necessary. What thoughts are being held onto that negate progress of any kind? What attributes need to be cultivated in order to serve the manifested request? Strength? Trust? All these areas need to be examined in the meantime.

Have you adequately prepared yourself for the treasures you await?

"Chance favors the prepared mind."

- Louis Pasteur

Authenticity

No one wants to be a hypocrite. We would like to be seen as genuine people, but more importantly, we want to see ourselves as being genuine. But what happens when the you- that-you-are-now and the you-that-you want-to-be are not yet the same person? Does that inherently make you a fraud?

If you are of the opinion that life is a series of lessons to be learned, then the description of fraud is highly inaccurate. Your spirit is on a quest to match up with your reality. When the two are disparate, uneasiness and discontent with life takes place. The merging of spiritual endeavors with experienced reality is crucial.

Quite often, many of us become stagnant in our pursuits for one reason or another. Instead of choosing to continue on our highest paths, some of us will make excuses for our inactivity.

The second we begin to do so, we lose our authenticity. We are refusing to acknowledge the truth of the matter.

The obstacles we encounter may be designed specifically to address those parts of our spirits which need development. It is through learning from these experiences, that we strengthen our characters and move closer to our desired situations. Spirit requires us to live and move within truth.

Authenticity is not only in the endpoint, but it is in the process. As long as progress is being made, then one can think of oneself as being genuine. Are you living an authentic life?

"The authentic self is the soul made visible."

- Sarah Ban Breathnach

The Beauty of Scars

Many of us bear physical scars that we try to hide. We conceal them with things such as clothing and cosmetics. If that does not suffice, we tend to position ourselves in such a way, so our wounds are out of sight.

On the other hand, how do we react when we see other people's scars? We may look in curiosity if our stares can go unnoticed. Sometimes, we may cringe and immediately look away. If the wound is undoubtedly noticeable, some of us feel more uneasy than the individual who bears the scar.

But what about our internal scars that no one can readily see? Is there any difference with our invisible imperfections? How often do we try to cover up our deepest emotional wounds from observers?

Some of us clothe ourselves with indifference, some with anger, and some with denial. But in many cases, our layers actually make our underlying issues that much more evident.

To live from one's spirit, scars must be acknowledged for what they truly are. To the ego, they are a blemish that indicates damaged goods. To spirit, a scar is nothing but proof of a problem encountered and dealt with. It's a reminder of one's strength and resilience.

Acknowledging them as such allows us to live unhindered and enables us to accept others more willingly. Recognizing our scars allows for complete healing.

How much of your true self are you hiding?

"Wisdom is scar tissue in disguise."

- unknown

Storybook Endings

As children, we are often amused by the tales we are told. As adults we choose the books we read and the movies we watch based upon what captures our attention. From mythology to contemporary news stories, it is clear that everyone enjoys a good story.

But in writing a good story, who is responsible for the final product? Is it the author, the editor, or are their roles completely intertwined?

 An author has to submit a decent manuscript before the editor can perform. The editor than makes the necessary revisions bringing that work to its highest potential. It is not the author's job to take care of the finishing details.

It is only required that the author dig deep inside and uncover a tale waiting to be told. The author relays that information to the best of his ability. In the end, he must be willing to allow the editor some freedom to cultivate a true work of art.

Is it any different with the way we live our lives?

Without our earnest contributions, the Universe has nothing of substance to work upon. On the other hand, how many of us try to take care of all the details when it's really not our place to do so? Are we allowing our "editor" to take care of things from its more knowledgeable perspective?

How are you contributing to the story of your life?

"There is no greater agony than bearing an untold story inside you."
- Maya Angelou

Buying Time

Cellular phones. Internet. Reality TV…the list is endless. The modern world is full of distractions and alternatives keep arising on a daily basis. Though many of these things make life easier and/or entertaining, they are generally used in excess of necessity.

The majority of us are consuming the time we have with meaningless activity. In doing so, we move further away from connecting with our spirits. Perhaps we need to re-evaluate the value of time. We always talk of "spending time" so perhaps we should think of it as being equivalent to money.

Currency can be used to purchase an item or it can also be used to secure an investment which may lead to future earnings.
Likewise, time can be used on a momentary pleasure and it, too, can be invested in activity that can lead to future rewards.

In finding the balance between these two options, we can start to treat time as the valued commodity it is.

Ask yourself if you would pay to engage in the activities with which you usually pass time. If the answer is no, that activity is essentially useless to you. Chances are it is working counteractively to any development of the spirit.

In order to connect with spirit it is imperative we disconnect from all the diversions. Wasting our time may cost us much more than we can imagine. Would you squander your money as you do your time?

"We say we waste time, but that is impossible. We waste ourselves."
- Alice Bloch

Acceptance

We've all experienced disappointment with the people closest to us. Often, our frustration with them has much more to do with our expectations of them not being met. It has little to do with their actual decisions or behaviors. Our emotional reactions to their choices sometimes get the best of us.

We have unfair expectations of the people in our lives. We forget that their spirit may be pulling them in a direction separate from ours. Of course with life-threatening decisions, as a concerned party we may feel the need to step in and offer them an alternate perspective. However, most of the things that annoy us about our loved ones have little to do with precarious situations.

We are often bothered by things that just don't go our way…our *expected* way.

Although we are the principal characters in each of our own stories, we sometimes forget that we also play supporting roles to the stories of others. Part of our spiritual growth involves allowing others to walk their own paths. Whether we agree with their choices or not, is irrelevant. We must respect their decisions.

We have to find it in our hearts to accept that they, too, have a journey. Looking from our point of view offers limited perspective on what their spiritual journeys require.

Are you supporting the people in your life, or are you blocking their paths for your own benefit?

"Love is the ability and willingness to allow those that you care for to be what they choose for themselves without any insistence that they satisfy you."

- Wayne Dyer

Thinking Big

It is not uncommon to meet with resistance when aspiring to greater heights. Some people will try to shield you from disappointment because they are genuinely concerned. Others will sway you from your goals simply out of spite.

Regardless of their individual reasons, all of these people will have one thing in common. They have settled for less in some, if not all, aspects of their lives and they feel you should do the same. At some point, they decided that their dreams were not worth their efforts.

Life can be additionally challenging when you decide to embark on a quest for more. Whether it's more money, better health, or more meaning, the road to abundance will be demanding. Though each of us has the capability to excel and shine, very few of us will take the opportunity to do so.

External support is helpful, but only the individuals with enough personal resolve will be able to meet this challenge head on. That resolve is a product of being in touch with one's spirit.

Spirit always requires us to aim high with our goals and ideals. It has no concept of limitation. Surrendering to the urge to settle for less is incomprehensible.

Things that are of true spiritual significance are not matters that should be settled upon. Don't you think you're worth the value of your dreams?

"There is no passion to be found playing small - in settling for a life that is less than the one you are capable of living."

- Nelson Mandela

Balancing Act

Our journeys can take us to some scary places. New adventures can be likened to walking on a tightrope. However, this particular tightrope tends to ascend with each step. It rarely stays level as we progress.

One problem with the tightrope is that it forces us to advance sequentially. There is no obvious way to get from point A to Z without taking most of the steps in between. We can not carelessly rush along its length and hope for the best. Our movements must be deliberate in nature.

In addition, the further we get from the starting point, the further we get from a place of solidity. And the nearer we get to the end, the further we have to fall. Even though the finishing point may be closer, we tend to feel increasing anxiety with each step because of greater potential loss.

The bottom line is that there is no real progress without some degree of risk. In many cases, the measure of the reward will be proportionate to the risk taken.

The Universe will accelerate us through some steps. But it will only rise to meet us once we move with purpose. The only guide to genuine purpose is listening closely to our spirits. Only spirit can indicate what amount of risk is acceptable.

Are you willing to risk the loss of support? Are you willing to temporarily lose the comfort of stability? What about the presence of vulnerability?

What risks are you truly willing to take for the rewards you seek?

"A ship is safe in harbor, but that's not what ships are for."
-William Shedd

Keeping It Real

What does it mean to become "real"?

Is it something that happens to us or something we each bring from within? The classic children's tale of "The Velveteen Rabbit" explores this very issue.

Written by Margery Williams in 1922, it tells the story of a toy rabbit's desire to become real. As the toy becomes favored by its owner, it begins to lose its original sheen. Despite its imperfections, the child loves this toy, and the toy now believes itself to be real.

Only when the toy encounters live rabbits does it begin to question itself once again. To its dismay, it is one day replaced as the favorite toy and is soon to be destroyed.

In waiting for its demise, the toy begins to review the little things that brought it joy. A miracle takes place, and in the end, the toy rabbit is transformed into the real being it always wanted to be.

How many of us wait to be made real by others? And what happens to our "realness" if those others are no longer associated with us?

Just like the toy rabbit, we often look to others for validation of our worthiness. It's only when we look inside and find the things that resonate with our souls, that our "realness" can rise to the surface.

From where does your sense of authenticity/realness originate?

"One's real life is often the life that one does not lead."

- Oscar Wilde

Déjà Vu

The rhythm of life dictates that all things are born, live, and then pass. We see the same pattern in observing the dawn giving way to the day eventually to be followed by sunset. Again, it is evident if we observe the changing of seasons. This pattern is the ultimate cycle.

But what about the smaller cycles we repeat during our lifetimes? When the phrase, "Why does this always happen to me?" is uttered, it is time for some serious reflection.

Very often we find ourselves in similar circumstances we've already experienced. Sometimes the names and faces of the characters around us have changed, but the same story plays on. We should regularly make time to closely examine our current situations to see if any echoes of the past persist.

Many times, these cycles are not forced upon us but we go through them *willingly*.

Though the circumstances may have been thrust upon us, the decisions we make in the midst of them are of our choosing.   Consequently, so is the outcome.

What if the universe works similarly to how we learn in school? We are repeatedly given the lesson until we can grasp the concept. Only then are we allowed to move on to the next lesson of increasing complexity.

Is the Universe trying to tell you something? Are there lessons you have been resistant to learning? What cycles are you unnecessarily repeating?

"To understand is to perceive patterns."

- Isaiah Berlin

Tunneling Through

Life is often challenging with unforeseen events taking place. The unexpected always forces us to review our basic set of beliefs. And if taken seriously and approached honestly, we are usually strengthened by the end of the trial.

But during the ordeal, we often feel the weight closing in on us from all sides. We burrow along hoping for a break in our circumstances, but it continues on with no relief in sight. There appears to be no proverbial light at the end of the tunnel.

Like in any excavation, hard work is required. Our true perspectives and motives must be unearthed before we can make any real progress.

Sometimes that progress is inhibited by things that are external. An individual or situation may be obscuring the light. There is no room to push the object to the side in order to advance. It must be dealt with and eliminated before you can see past it.

At other times, our vision is obscured due to our own blindfolds. There is nothing in our way except our selves. We have to acknowledge our resistance to seeing things as they are.

Most often, our difficulty is exaggerated by something completely internal…our inability to have faith. How do you look for a light that you don't believe is there in the first place?

What is the source of your tunnel-vision?

"You can't have a light without a dark to stick it in."

- Arlo Guthrie

Collective Soul

We often become so involved in our daily challenges that we forget we belong to a much larger picture. Most of us operate as if we are disconnected from the world at large. It becomes easy to believe that our words and actions bear consequences only for ourselves and those with whom we are in immediate contact.

But a quick look at the world outside of our selves reveals otherwise. Whether or not we consciously recognize it, on some level we are all connected.

It's the reason we smile at uplifting stories that have nothing to do with us. And it's also the reason we feel the pain of strangers enduring some sort of tragedy.

There is a collective soul that encompasses each of our own. Think of all souls on the earth represented as an infinite body of water. Individually, we may only be one drop in an ocean, but it is worthwhile to remember that even single drops make ripples.

Note that the ripples continue further on a molecular level that we are unable to see with our eyes.

Perhaps the same is true of our actions that we believe to be insignificant. Their effects continue on despite our inability to observe firsthand.

There is a domino effect for whatever energy we project onto the world around us. Positivity can radiate outward as easily as negativity.

How have you been choosing to contribute to the collective soul?

"Remember there's no such thing as a small act of kindness. Every act creates a ripple with no logical end"

- Scott Adams

Open Spaces

Tuning in to spirit isn't always so easy. Many of us fail to do so because of the many distractions that life provides. However, when we do take time for self evaluation, we may not even be aware of where to start.

Individuals well acquainted with meditation easily connect with their inner selves. They also use this tool to restore balance if deemed necessary. However, relatively few of us take consistent time out for this practice. How can we evaluate our spiritual states? What other indicators exist?

Very often, our physical spaces mirror our mental spaces and therefore reflect our spiritual states.

How many of us live with constant disorganization and clutter? Perhaps we're overwhelmed by all that needs to be done in order to improve our surroundings. Such spaces tend to weaken us instead of rejuvenating us.

Creating a peaceful space to escape the hectic nature of everyday life is essential. The wellness of spirit depends on it. There should be at least one area which allows you to exhale as you enter it. It should serve as a physical and mental retreat.

Meditation works directly from the inside. If this practice is not yet feasible, try working from the outside in. Clearing your physical space will allow you to redirect your energies. As a result your mental load lightens thereby creating room for spirit to emerge.

Assuming this to be true, what do your surroundings say about the current state of your spirit?

"Just as a picture is drawn by an artist, surroundings are created by the activities of the mind."

- unknown

Growing Pains

"No pain, no gain."

We're all familiar with this overused saying. But do we really take it heart?

Usually we think of pain in physical terms and we attach negative traits to it such as suffering. But the pains that take place during voluntary spiritual growth need not be distressful.

Perhaps a more accurate choice of word is discomfort. There is some degree of uneasiness involved when taking anything to the next level. Seldom do great personal advances come about without it.

There are talents in each one of us that remain uncovered simply because we never thought of trying. Foreign undertakings can be frightening, but we have to remember that spirit thrives on new challenges.

Facing the unfamiliar is a prerequisite to bettering ourselves. And more often than not, our anticipation far exceeds the reality of the situation.

Accepting the uneasiness and recognizing it as a necessary component for progress should lessen the perception of fear.

Like the athlete in training, stretching out those never-before-used muscles will initially be uncomfortable. However, the end result is movement you once may have thought impossible.

"Pain is weakness leaving the body."

- Tom Sobal

Illogical Conclusions

There is much talk about the left brain versus the right brain. Logic versus creativity and intuition. What happens when these two sides meet up?

All too often, our "left-brained activity" can interfere with our quest for spiritual growth. The mystical nature of our relationships with the Universe does not fit into a tidy explanation. The concept of quantum physics appears to be the closest explanation we have, but even it makes little sense by the typical standards of science.

Generally speaking, people tend to discount what they can not understand. Unfortunately, many of the concepts that spirituality embraces are abstract.

For example, a popular concept is "The Law of Attraction." Simply put, your thoughts become your reality. An individual who seeks definitive proof for this before succumbing to it, may be sorely disappointed.

Truth can be validated by experience, but you can't have the experience if you don't believe in it in the first place.

Sometimes we just have to have trust in the wisdom of the Universe. Being able to comprehend the details of phenomena does not make it any more authentic.

Most of us do not understand the molecular structure of oxygen or how it is transported and utilized in our bodies, but that doesn't mean we can't breathe. Our benefit from it is not dependent on our comprehension.

Don't get hung up on being unable to figure every thing out. Believing in the magic of the Universe is more important than being able to understand it.

"Pure logic is the ruin of the spirit."

- Antoine de Saint-Exupery

Hidden Beliefs

To be truly in touch with spirit, we must know ourselves inside out. There is no room for unconscious thoughts that work against us in the pursuit of bettering ourselves. We may consciously think of ourselves in one way, but we must make sure our underlying beliefs are supportive. If not, we place ourselves in losing situations.

For example, a person can believe that he is a good individual. This appears to be a positive belief and on its own, it is. However, the same person can believe that "good guys always come last." So what does this say about the probable outcome for any of his future endeavors?

If what you believe is what you manifest, then your shrouded beliefs become that much more significant. Your self image is composed of your conscious and unconscious notions of who you are. Your ability to do better for yourself is based upon that self image.

In assessing our self images, we must be as objective as possible. We may not want to initially admit to some of the beliefs that we have because we may view them as negative or weak.

Only when we are honest with ourselves, can we begin to ascend. Even when we think we know ourselves, we must occasionally re-evaluate because we change with time and experience. Our beliefs need revision or we will continue to act in ways that reinforce a previously existing self-image.

What do you truly believe about yourself? Are those beliefs helping you to rise or are they standing in your way?

"Most of the shadows of this life are caused by our standing in our own sunshine."

- Ralph Waldo Emerson

Waiting to Bloom

It is said that much of life is spent waiting for the next thing to happen. In times of stagnancy, it can be difficult to see the relevance of the waiting period. Waiting implies we exist in a passive state. This need not be the case.

Many of us wait to be picked in order to move to the next level. Some of us wait for employers to grant us promotions. Others of us wait for chance to give us significant others. Many will wait for the gift of children. But in the meantime, little attention is given to nurturing our own spiritual progress. We believe if we obtain those other things, then we can begin to center ourselves and settle into life.

We ask the Universe why it is tormenting us instead of us understanding and accepting that the "waiting" period is necessary. Perhaps we are not the ones doing the waiting. Perhaps the Universe is the one waiting on us to rise.

We forget that the world will give us the essential conditions in order for us to obtain what is necessary. In prematurely granting us the things we say that we want, attention may be taken away from cultivating the things that we need.

Envision a flower growing in nature. A person picks the flower and transplants it to a vase indoors. Soon after its transfer, the flower begins to fade and eventually dies. What can we learn from this?

Sometimes a flower has to be left in place in order to reach its full bloom. Are you facilitating or hindering your own budding potential?

"And the day came when the risk to remain tight in a bud was more painful than the risk it took to blossom."

- Anais Nin

Journeys

Life is often compared to the proverbial journey. We know that we must go on this ride, but how many of us are paying attention to our method of travel?

In literal journeys, some of us will prefer to fly. We simply wish to get from point A to point B without thought. We do not care to take part in the details of the entire experience. We assume the pilot will take us where we want to go.

Others of us will choose to travel long distances by train. From this vantage point, we can observe more of the experience. We see more details than those in flight. However, we still do not want to be held accountable for our movement. We abdicate responsibility to the conductor, just as others do to the pilot.

Some will decide they prefer to walk alone. They witness each excruciating detail of their journey and are not accepting of offered assistance. They often place unnecessary burden upon their selves.

The conscious individual probably approaches life like a road trip. Sometimes they sit back and ride during the unexpected twists and turns in unfamiliar territory. Other times they instinctively take initiative and lead their own course. They are willing to be accountable for the consequences of their travels, yet they recognize the presence of a greater force at times of uncertainty.

In the beginning, the journey may seem daunting. How you choose to navigate makes all the difference to how you experience it.

"Too often we are so preoccupied with the destination, we forget the journey."

-unknown

Stuck

We've all had the experience of running into temporary obstructions. Getting stuck in the mud is really no different than any of life's challenges.

Option number one is to take the emotional route and let the situation get the best of you. Your energy is invested in complaining and not in actually finding and contributing to a solution. All you can do is hope for a miracle. Resolution is possible, but you have effectively removed yourself from the equation.

Option number two is attempting to fix your problem. Turning the wheels in a slightly different direction before you proceed may be all that is required. If you're still not free, you can choose to get out of the vehicle and do the work necessary. It will be messy, but at least your actions will prove to be constructive. If that's still not enough, you can ask for assistance from others. One way or another, you will get yourself out of the situation.

Option number three is to get another vehicle. It's not necessarily giving up if an accurate assessment of the situation has been made. Just perhaps, the vehicle you were driving in was inappropriate for the route you were on. The important thing is not to blame the vehicle but recognize and accept it was your choice to drive it in the first place.

Spirit works most effectively within the two latter options. It will lead you to the most suitable one for your particular circumstances. The trick is to be aware enough to make a conscious decision.

How are you choosing to deal with your obstacles?

"Life is full of obstacle illusions."

- Grant Frazier

Insincerity

Many of us deal with manipulative people. Whether it is at a job or within our families, we often encounter individuals with agendas. Sometimes, *we're* the ones with agendas.

It is important to remember not to get caught up in playing the game. It's even more important to recognize why we and others engage in this behavior in the first place.

Whenever we approach someone with an agenda, we end up playing a role in hopes of getting what we want. When we interact with others through this role, we are neglecting the reality of who we really are.

In a way, we are rejecting our spirit. We choose to act from behind pretense because we are fearful that our real self is not enough.

Attempting to navigate by any measure of deceitfulness works against you. It doesn't matter what the situation is.

It could be about business or it could be about love. Like eventually attracts like.

Whenever at least one party approaches the other insincerely, the consequences will not be favorable. Even if something positive appears to come out of it, chances are it will be short-lived. Only when you move through the world as truth, does it leave room for the Universe to incorporate its positive influence.

Spirit always shows its true face. It has no reason to hide behind facades. Do you?

"Authentic treachery is found when we abandon ourselves, becoming deaf to the whispers of our spirits and blind to the powerful potential therein."

- Joaquin Mariel Espinosa

Human Relations

In walking through our daily routines, it is likely that we tend to keep the same company. Not only do we encounter the same characters, but we tend to relate to each other in the customary way. Whether it is family, friends, or co-workers, we tend to unconsciously interact out of habit.

We often relegate people to the roles we believe they play in our lives i.e. the girl behind the counter who serves coffee or the man who gives us the paper every morning. We even treat people we spend more time with in the same detached manner.

If we keep in mind that spirit requires new experiences to continually elevate, then it stands to reason that having the same interactions with the same people does not lend itself to bettering ourselves. Either we need to incorporate some new people into our circles, or we need to change the nature of our present interactions. Better yet, both strategies may be employed.

When we welcome new individuals in, we are exposed to new perspectives and new ideas.

Our existence becomes less biased by our own tainted view of the world. As a result, our spirit is less constricted.

When interacting with familiar people in new ways, even making deliberate eye contact is a huge change. It's not possible to have in-depth conversations with everyone, however, just infusing a smile or glance with positivity has the potential to radiate beyond the receiver. No time is too brief for the influence of spirit.

Are you relating to people through spirit or through routine?

"When two people relate to each other authentically and humanly, God is the electricity that surges between them."

-Martin Buber

Inner Light

Discussions about spirit and spirituality are often abstract and challenging for many people to understand. It can bring about uneasiness in those not prepared to talk about it. It can also be uncomfortable for those who practice it in private, but are hesitant to share their points of view.

Making an intangible concept something more concrete lends itself to a better understanding for each of us.

Quite possibly the most visual reference we have for spirit is the use of the phrase "the light within". It is one that we instinctively understand. In using this analogy, the mysterious nature of spirit is made less so.

Each of us enters this world with an innate light. In an ideal situation, we are surrounded by people, family and friends, who nurture this light. We may also have activities in our lives that seem to strengthen it.

Other activities tend to dim it. In our daily choices, we should consider how our radiance is affected. This is our personal spiritual experience.

We must also take into consideration how we affect other people. When we come into contact with others we can sustain, re-kindle, or diminish their inner lights. If we consider how much power our words and actions really have, perhaps we would be more careful in how we interact. This is our interpersonal spiritual experience.

Spirituality really comes down to one question. Have you been cultivating or extinguishing the light within?

"People are like stained-glass windows. They sparkle and shine when the sun is out, but when the darkness sets in, their true beauty is revealed only if there is a light from within."

- Elisabeth Kubler-Ross

Doing the Work

As spiritual beings, it is our right to dream big. If we truly believe that we are derived from an all-encompassing source, then having small aspirations or none at all should be unacceptable.

Though we have the potential for miraculous things to happen, it is not to say that we should sit back and expect for every dream to come to realization without our active participation. In honor of the Universe that supports us, we should act in anticipation of its assistance. We should also embrace any difficulties along the way instead of asking, "Why me?"

We often long for the fruits of our labor without going through the actual labor. Sometimes the work involved is physical. Sometimes it is intellectual or spiritual. It may require us to raise our standards and strive for areas well past our previous limitations.

It is not easy to break through well established boundaries. It is not easy to move towards goals that appear unattainable. It is not always easy to choose the most virtuous route. But true elevation challenges us in this way. Without it, life becomes mundane. Treasures become meaningless.

It is imperative that we respect the "struggles" that go along with our victories. In becoming more spiritual individuals, the so-called "struggles" simply become a part of the process. Like a detour in the road, we navigate around them instead of resisting them, denying them, or turning back. There is acknowledgement and acceptance of the blockage and continued forward motion.

Do you accept your trials as necessary or are you avoiding the effort your dreams require of you?

"He who wants a rose must respect the thorn."

- Persian Proverb

The Importance of Doubt

We have all thought some feat impossible to achieve at one point in life or another. Perhaps it was passing an impossible class in school. Maybe it was coming out first place in a competition or dreaming of opening up a business. Whatever the deed, there has certainly been a time when something appeared unachievable.

Being plagued with doubt seems to be an affliction of the more mature. Babies do whatever comes naturally to them. They grab at everything, make noise at "inappropriate" times, and have the audacity to start walking. They don't read manuals, or wait for instruction. They just *do*.

The youngest of us keep pursuing "impossible" tasks despite frequent failure. Failed attempts don't even register as being unsuccessful. Babies are resolute in their missions. Doubt does not exist in their limited vocabularies. But perhaps the presence of doubt is not needed in such young lives.

So what if doubt actually has a purposeful role in our lives?

First of all, doubt indicates some level of humility. To be completely without it may point towards arrogance. When working with and believing in spirit, one becomes assured. When believing in it is not necessary, one becomes arrogant.

Second, any doubt that appears is transient and serves as a reminder to call on spirit. Fixating on it paralyzes our actions. Recognizing it can actually empower us.

Lastly, doubt is an indication that the next level is being approached. Often, it speaks loudest when we are on the verge of standing out.

Do you use the feeling of doubt to drive you or drown you?

"Any belief worth having must survive doubt."

- unknown

Glory Days

We all have memories that we cherish. Special people have come and gone in our lives and miraculous moments have passed that will never be forgotten. On a bleak day, these sorts of remembrances can help brighten up our moods.

However, many of us tend to dwell in the past. We remember things like the carelessness of youth and wish for its return. We complain about our current physical condition and remember when our health was optimal. We remember our dreams in times before life brought occasional disappointment.

We often say things such as "Those were the *best* years of my life..." Commonly referred to as "glory days", our nostalgic recollections tend to blur out any rough spots.

Understand that every time you utter that phrase is to deny the potential of every moment thereafter. It is an unconscious declaration that nothing will ever be better.

It serves as an excuse not to reach for anything higher. If we have the mindset that the best has already passed, why try?

When we find ourselves within that particular frame of mind, it is time to re-evaluate where we see ourselves heading. Are we stuck glorifying the past? Are we holding the same intentions and ideals that we held twenty years ago? If the answer is yes, then we are probably not in line with spirit.

Life keeps evolving and so should our perspectives. As we gain experience it is likely that our goals and objectives may need revision. By aligning ourselves with these new standards, we reach for the next set of pleasures that come along with that. We shouldn't only seek happiness in the past.

Spirit's aim is to keep growing. Are you?

"If we're growing, we're always going to be out of our comfort zone."
- John Maxwell

Windswept

For many of us, it is difficult to imagine that something greater is at work. For those of us that do believe, we often have difficulty *remembering* that something bigger than ourselves is out there. Believing in the unseen requires an enormous amount of faith. Perhaps if we liken the nature of the Universe to the nature of wind, this belief becomes more concrete.

We have no control over the wind's appearance. It comes whether we are prepared for it or not. It can appear as a gentle breeze or a tumultuous current that forces us in a specific direction. It has whimsical nature and can change direction without warning. We never see the wind directly, but we see its effects and therefore believe in it. The same is true of the way life works. We can't see the force that works around us, but we often feel its effects.

If we look in the physical world, we see that that a simple motion can generate electricity. To witness a windmill slowly turning in the distance looks quite peaceful.

One can almost forget that tremendous amounts of power are being generated. The "nothing-ness" of wind is being transformed into something tangible (electricity).

We can apply this principle to our own lives. When it appears that nothing is happening, we have to believe that greater forces are at work. We need only to attune ourselves to the direction our winds are blowing in order to harness the potential energy that is being created around us. Our own "nothing-ness" has the ability to be transformed.

Let the touch of wind serve as a reminder of greater forces unseen. Like a plane uses a tail wind to get further in less time, we can use the currents in our lives to fulfill the intentions of spirit - in less time with fewer struggles. Are you working with your wind or against it?

"I can't change the direction of the wind, but I can adjust my sails to always reach my destination."

- Jimmy Dean

Fine Dining

"Keep your eyes on your own plate."

Dining etiquette dictates that it is inappropriate to stare at other people's food. It would be even more inappropriate to reach over and begin to eat from another person's plate. Perhaps we can take a spiritual cue from this edict.

It is human nature to be somewhat curious about what is going on around you. It is also human nature to occasionally compare oneself to the next person. However, it is ego's nature to obsess on the good fortune of others. It is also the ego's nature to want to take what the next person has.

Ego greedily looks left and right. It thrives on comparison and competition. It literally can not exist without these elements. Coveting what someone else is working with does nothing to help your own progress. It is wasted energy.

Spirit recognizes the limitless potential of any given situation.

It does not dwell on the fact that it lacks what the next individual has. Spirit isn't acquainted with the concept of "lack". In fact, it acknowledges the greatness in others while pursuing its own path to greatness. Spirit acknowledges that *everyone* is worthy of rewards.

Someone else's plate may appear more appetizing, but in pursuing what is not ours we may never savor the Universal offerings possible for each of us.

What is for you is for **you**. If you truly believe that, it's easier to keep your eyes on your own plate.

Where has your focus been?

"Your life is yours and yours alone. Rise up and live it."
- Terry Goodkind

Nature's Lessons

Wisdom can be found all around us. It can be through the words of a stranger or the actions of a friend, but most wisdom comes from simple observation - especially when observing nature itself.

We can gain insight into our own lives by paying close attention to the most seemingly insignificant happenings. For instance, when was the last time you gave any thought to spiders?

They're usually portrayed as dangerous and cunning. In reality, most pose little risk to humans. However, their existence can be helpful in illustrating how we need to approach our own lives.

Spiders have the ability to create an intricate web using only what they have inside of them. When they create that first thread they rely on the wind to carry it to an appropriate surface to continue the process. After expending the energy needed to construct their immediate world, they sit back and wait for their web to capture the nourishment they need.

The spider knows when something has been caught because of the vibrations that travel through its creation.

In a spiritual context, we can approach life similarly. We have to reach within ourselves to order the world around us. We can take initial action then wait for the "winds of possibility" to further our efforts. Having been helped by the Universe, we can continue to build with confidence. Once finished, we can wait for subtle vibrations that indicate the capture of our intended goals.

The next time you see a spider or its web, be reminded of the power you hold to create the world around you.

What have you set your own web to trap?

"Nature is just enough; but men and women must comprehend and accept her suggestions."

- Antoinette Brown Blackwell

Mixed Signals

Part of the human drama is battling our conflicting nature. We say one thing and do another. We even tell our children, "Do as I say, not as I do." Instead of working to correct it, we seem to willingly accept what we know to be a shortcoming.

If we believe that the discrepancies amongst our words and actions are acceptable, then we are doing a great disservice to our selves. Personal growth is reflected by having integrity. Not only is the alignment of our thoughts, words, and actions important to self perception (i.e. how we see ourselves), it is equally important to how the Universe sees us.

We have to consider the Universe as an accomplice as we navigate through life. Just as we would do with any other partner, we have to be explicit in what each of our obligations are and what we expect from one another. Otherwise, the partnership is hopeless. How can anyone assist you if you are not clear on what you want?

The Universe awaits our signals just as we wait for the light at an intersection. A working light should not display red and green at the same time. In the same way, our actions and words should not contradict each other.

The primary way a traffic light malfunctions is from disruption of its power source. A disconnection from our power source of spirit challenges our integrity. This results in the breakdown of our own signals to the world around us.

The Universe is waiting upon your direction. Are you sending mixed signals?

"It is as if the ordinary language we use every day has a hidden set of signals; a kind of secret code."

— William Stafford

#1647 3832333

ISBN 1425177765-4

9 781425 177652